HI!

Elizabeth Claire

MINERVA BOOKS, LTD.
30 West 26th Street, New York, N.Y. 10010

HI! was written and field-tested with the cooperation
of the Fort Lee Public School System, Fort Lee,
New Jersey, Alan W. Sugarman, Superintendent.

Copyright © 1985 by
Elizabeth Claire

All rights reserved, including the right of
reproduction in whole or in part in any form.

Published by
MINERVA BOOKS, LTD.
30 West 26th Street
New York, N.Y. 10010

Manufactured in the United States of America

ISBN: 0-8056-0122-8

10 9 8 7 6 5 4 3

CONTENTS

	Page
Hi, hello, so long, goodbye.	5
The alphabet.	7
What is it?	9
Match	10
What is it?	11
World Map: Where are you from?	12
What is your name?	13
Numbers 0–10	15
Numbers 11–20	16
Good morning, afternoon, Mr, Mrs., Miss	17
Things in school	18
May I have a pencil, please?	19
Match: things we need	20
What's your last name	21
Listen	22
In the classroom	24
Match: things in the classroom	25
More things in the classroom	26
Listen (Go)	27
BINGO: things in the classroom	28
How are you?	29
Places in school	30
May I go to the. . . ?	31
Listen: at the blackboard	32
Game: go to the office	34
Colors	35
Listen (Don't ——)	38
Listen and read (test)	40
The face	41
The body	43
Puzzle: parts of the body	45
BINGO: parts of the body	46
Singular and plural	47
Match: parts of the body	48
ABC order	50
Writing numbers	53
What time is it?	56

	Page
The calendar	59
The days of the week	60
Make a calendar	61
Review	62
Questions and answers	63
Address a letter	65
Match: things in the classroom	66
Listen	67
What do you see?	68
Listen	70
More questions and answers	71
Write about yourself	74
How are you?	75
Pronouns	77
Am, Is, Are	78
Yes, I am; no, I'm not	79
Toys	80
Singular or plural: test	81
What do you have?	82
How many?	83
Do you have_____?	84
Milly's family	86
This is my family	87
Ask questions	88
Write about a boy (he & his)	89
Write about a girl (she & her)	90
Listen	91
More numbers	92
Money	93
Coins: how much is it?	95
Conversation review	96
Review	97
Review: sentence structure	100
Review: vocabulary	101
Write a story	102
Be polite	103
The Flag Salute, America	104

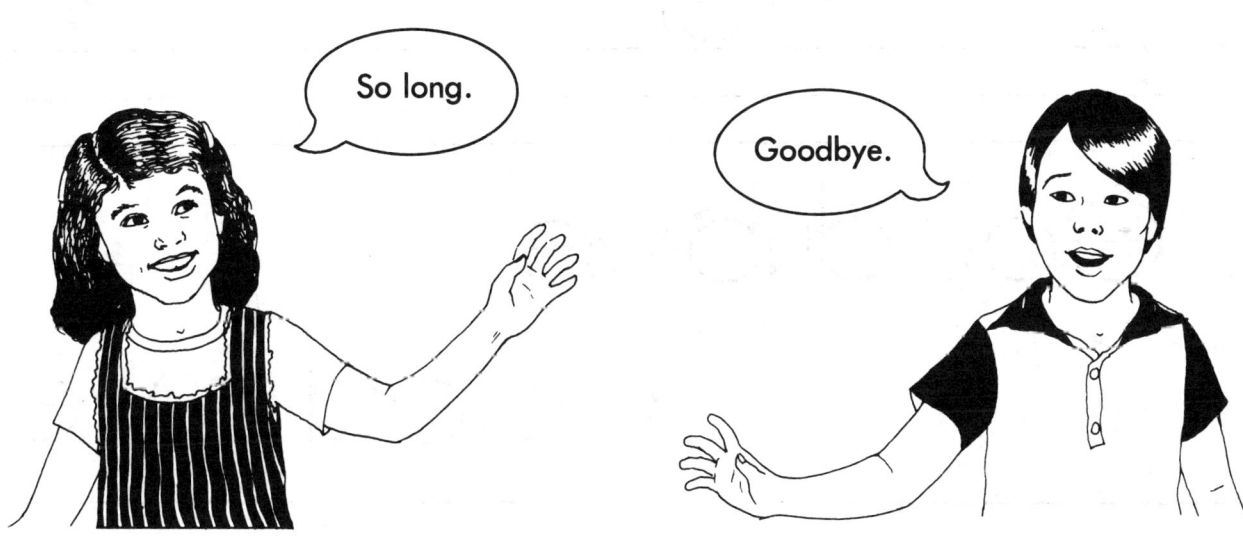

Copy:

1. Hi Hi Hi Hi

2. Hello Hello Hello

3. So long So long

4. Good bye

   Good bye

THE ALPHABET

CAPITAL LETTERS
A B C D E F G H I J K L M N O P Q R S T U V W X Y Z
COPY the capital letters:

A _____ B _____ C _____

D _____ E _____ F _____

G _____ H _____ I _____

J _____ K _____ L _____

M _____ N _____ O _____

P _____ Q _____ R _____

S _____ T _____ U _____

V _____ W _____ X _____

Y _____ Z _____

SMALL LETTERS
a b c d e f g h i j k l m n o p q r s t u v w x y z
COPY the small letters:

a _____ b _____ c _____

d _____ e _____ f _____

g _____ h _____ i _____

j _____ k _____ l _____

m _____ n _____ o _____

p _____ q _____ r _____

s _____ t _____ u _____

v _____ w _____ x _____

y _____ z _____

WHAT IS IT?

Draw a line from A to B to C to D . . .

A B C D E F G H I J K L M N O P Q R S T U V W X Y Z

It is a _____.

MATCH

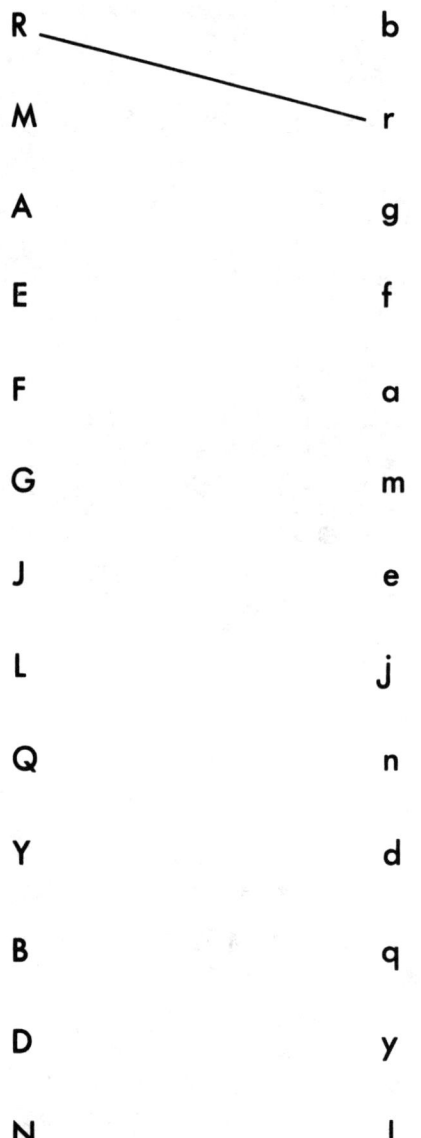

WHAT IS IT?

Draw a line from a to b to c to d . . .

a b c d e f g h i j k l m n o p q r s t u v w x y z

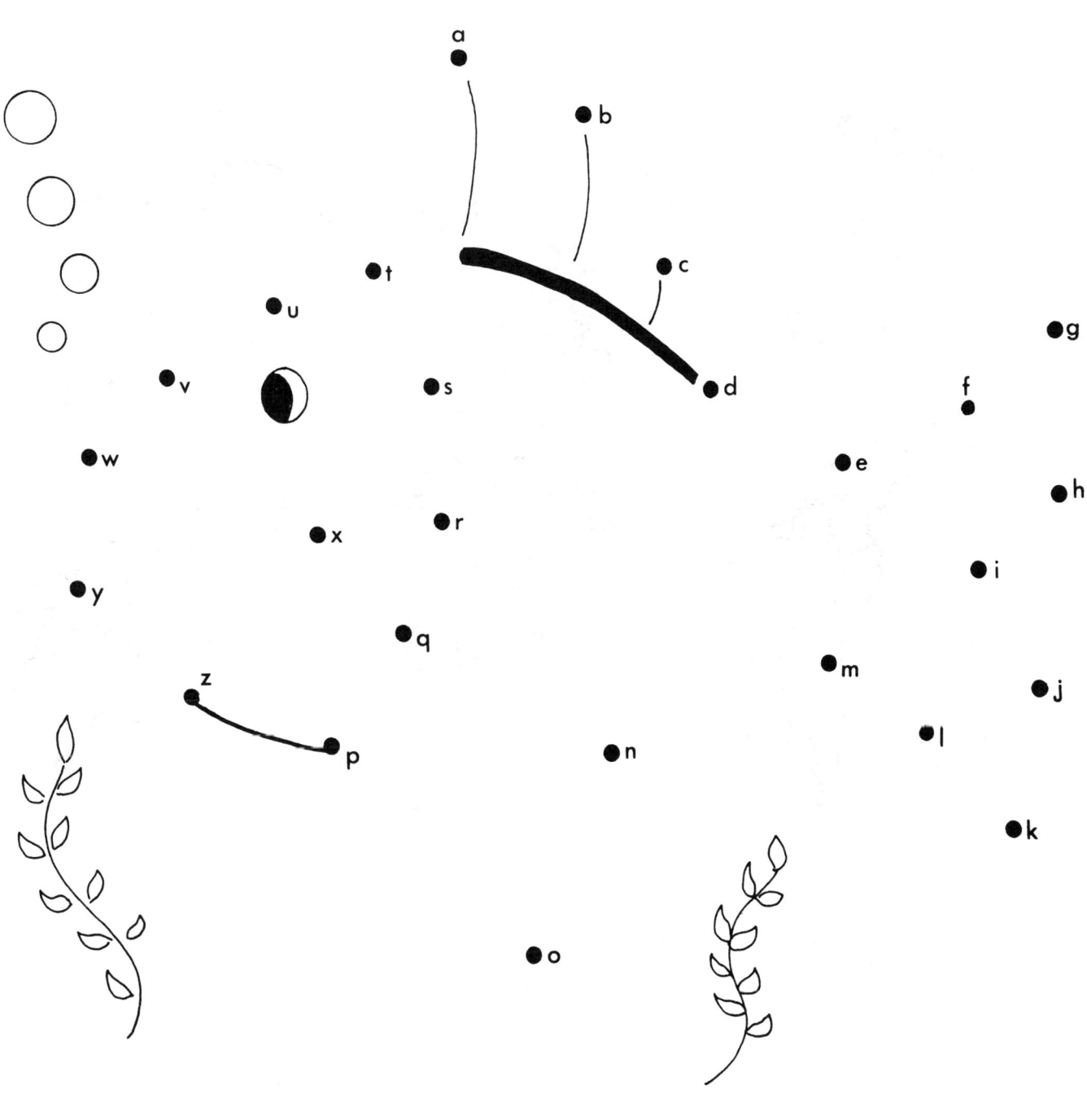

It's a _____.

FIND THE UNITED STATES.   **FIND YOUR COUNTRY.**

Where are you from? _____

12

| What's = <u>What is</u>   I'm = <u>I am</u> |

Copy:

1. What's your name?

2. My name is

3. Where are you from?

4. I'm from

NUMBERS

> COUNT:
> 0 1 2 3 4 5 6 7 8 9 10

Say the numbers:

a. 3 0 2 5 8 6 1 9 4 7 10

b. 4 2 1 0 8 6 7 9 10 3 5

c. 1 10 3 5 2 8 7 0 9 6 5 4

Sing:

1 little, 2 little, 3 little Indians,
4 little, 5 little, 6 little Indians,
7 little, 8 little, 9 little Indians,
10 little Indian boys.

Write the numbers the teacher says:

___ ___ ___ ___ ___ ___ ___ ___ ___ ___

___ ___ ___ ___ ___ ___ ___ ___ ___ ___

___ ___ ___ ___ ___ ___ ___ ___ ___ ___

MORE NUMBERS

> COUNT:
> 11 12 13 14 15 16 17 18 19 20

Say the numbers:

d. 12 3 11 5 8 13 9 14 7 20 0

e. 0 14 11 12 17 19 20 6 2 18 13

f. 20 16 19 17 14 0 11 13 15 12 10

g. 12 17 19 13 20 6 14 7 18 15 11

h. 19 17 15 20 13 11 12 18 16 14 3

i. 20 11 15 13 19 14 17 18 12 17 5

Write the numbers the teacher says:

___ ___ ___ ___ ___ ___ ___ ___ ___

___ ___ ___ ___ ___ ___ ___ ___ ___

___ ___ ___ ___ ___ ___ ___ ___ ___

Copy:
Good morning. _____

Good afternoon. _____

See you tomorrow. _____

THINGS IN SCHOOL

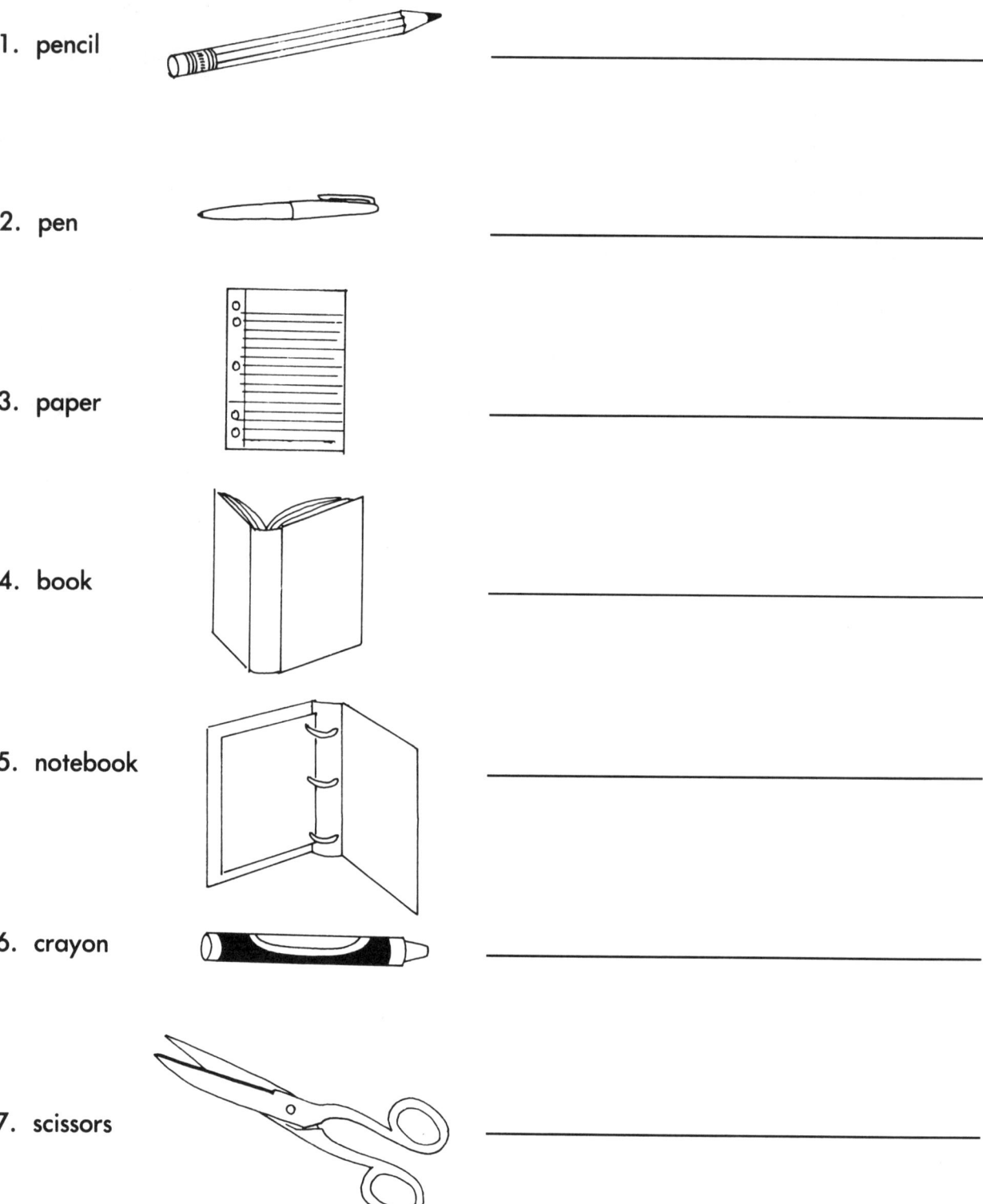

1. pencil _____

2. pen _____

3. paper _____

4. book _____

5. notebook _____

6. crayon _____

7. scissors _____

Read:

1. May I have a pencil, please?

2. May I have a pen, please?

3. May I have a book, please?

4. May I have a paper, please?*

5. May I have crayons, please?*

6. May I have scissors, please?*

7. Thank you.

8. You're welcome.

*To the teacher: The above forms are correct, simple English, selected to help communicative competence of the total beginner. You may teach the more native-sounding "May I have a *piece* of paper, *pair* of scissors, and *some* crayons" if you prefer.

MATCH

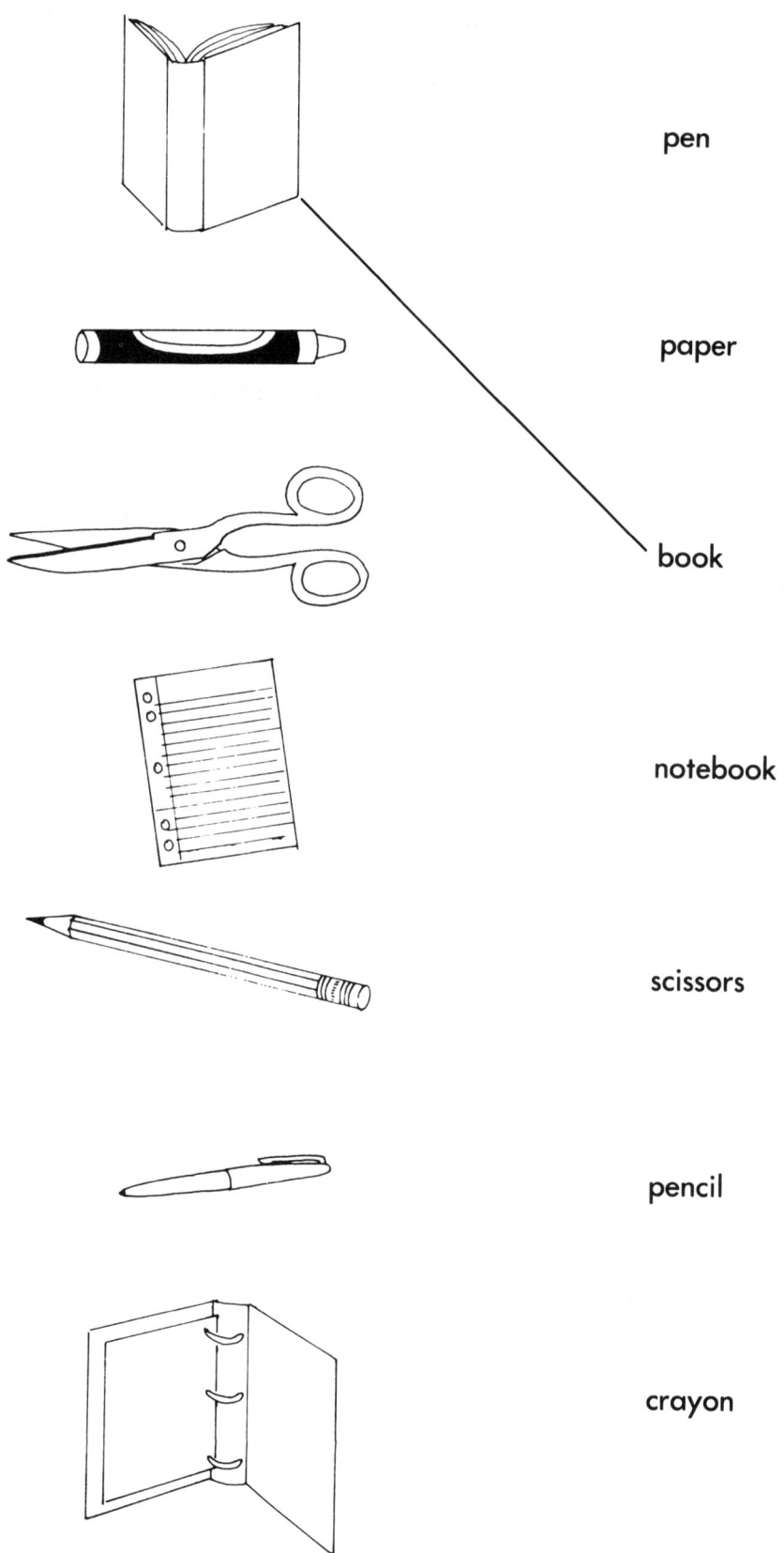

pen

paper

book

notebook

scissors

pencil

crayon

1. What's your last name?
   My last name is Blanco.

2. What's your last name?
   My last name is Kato.

3. What's your last name?
   My last name is Baker.

Copy:

1. What's your last name?

2. My last name is

 # LISTEN

1. up

2. down

3. hand

4. mouth

5. eyes

6. Stand up.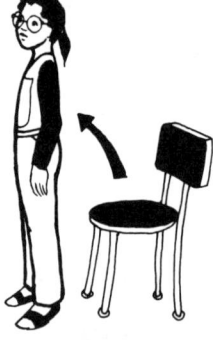

7. Sit down.

8. Raise your hand.

9. Put your hand down.

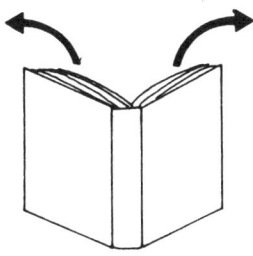

10. Open your book.

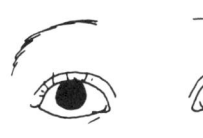

13. Open your eyes.

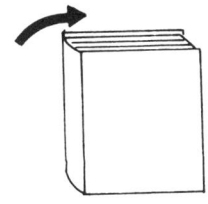

11. Close your book.

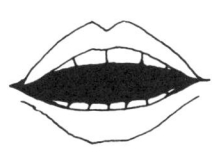

14. Open your mouth.

12. Close your eyes.

15. Close your mouth.

23

IN THE CLASSROOM

Copy:

1. teacher

2. children

3. boy

4. girl

5. chair

6. desk

7. table

8. door

9. window

10. blackboard

MATCH

1. window

2. teacher

3. boy

4. blackboard

5. desk

6. table

7. chair

8. door

9. girl

10. children

Copy:

11. flag

12. map

13. calendar

14. clock

15. picture

16. chalk

17. eraser

18. dictionary

19. ruler

20. floor

LISTEN

1. Stand up.

2. Put your chair under your desk.

3. Go to the blackboard.

4. Go to the door.

5. Go to the window.

6. Go to the map.

7. Go to the calendar.

8. Go to the wastebasket.

9. Go to the table.

B I N G O

		FREE		

Write one word in each square. Mix the order of the words so that everyone's bingo card is different. Cover the words that the teacher says. When you have five words in a row, say "BINGO!"

book	chair	eraser	boy
pen	pencil	paper	desk
table	flag	calendar	map
dictionary	chalk	blackboard	girl
teacher	children	picture	ruler
clock	window	door	floor

Copy:

1. How are you?

2. I'm fine, thankyou.

PLACES IN SCHOOL

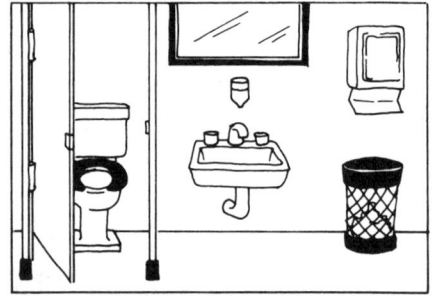

1. Bathroom

2. Office

3. Gym

5. Library

6. Lunchroom

7. Class

8. ESL Class

9. Auditorium

LISTEN

1. Stand up.

2. Put your chair under your desk.

3. Go to the blackboard.

4. Write your name.
   Write your last name. Jack Bak-

5. Write "A, B, C, D." ABCD

6. Write the numbers. 1 2 3 4 5 6 7 8 9 10

7. Write B-O-Y. BO

8. Write G-I-R-L. GIR

9. Draw a line under your name. <u>Jack</u>

10. Draw a line under A, B, C, D. <u>ABCD</u>

11. Draw a line under 3.   1 2 <u>3</u> 4 5

12. Draw a line under BOY.   <u>BOY</u>

13. Draw a circle around your last name.   Jack (Baker)

14. Draw a circle around 6.   1 2 3 4 5 (6) 7

15. Draw a circle around GIRL.   (GIRL)

16. Draw a circle around ABCD.   (ABCD)

17. Erase your name.

18. Erase 7.

19. Erase BOY.

20. Erase everything.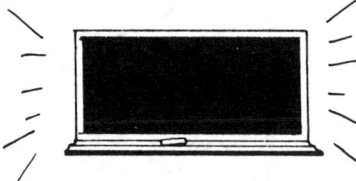

GAME: GO TO THE OFFICE

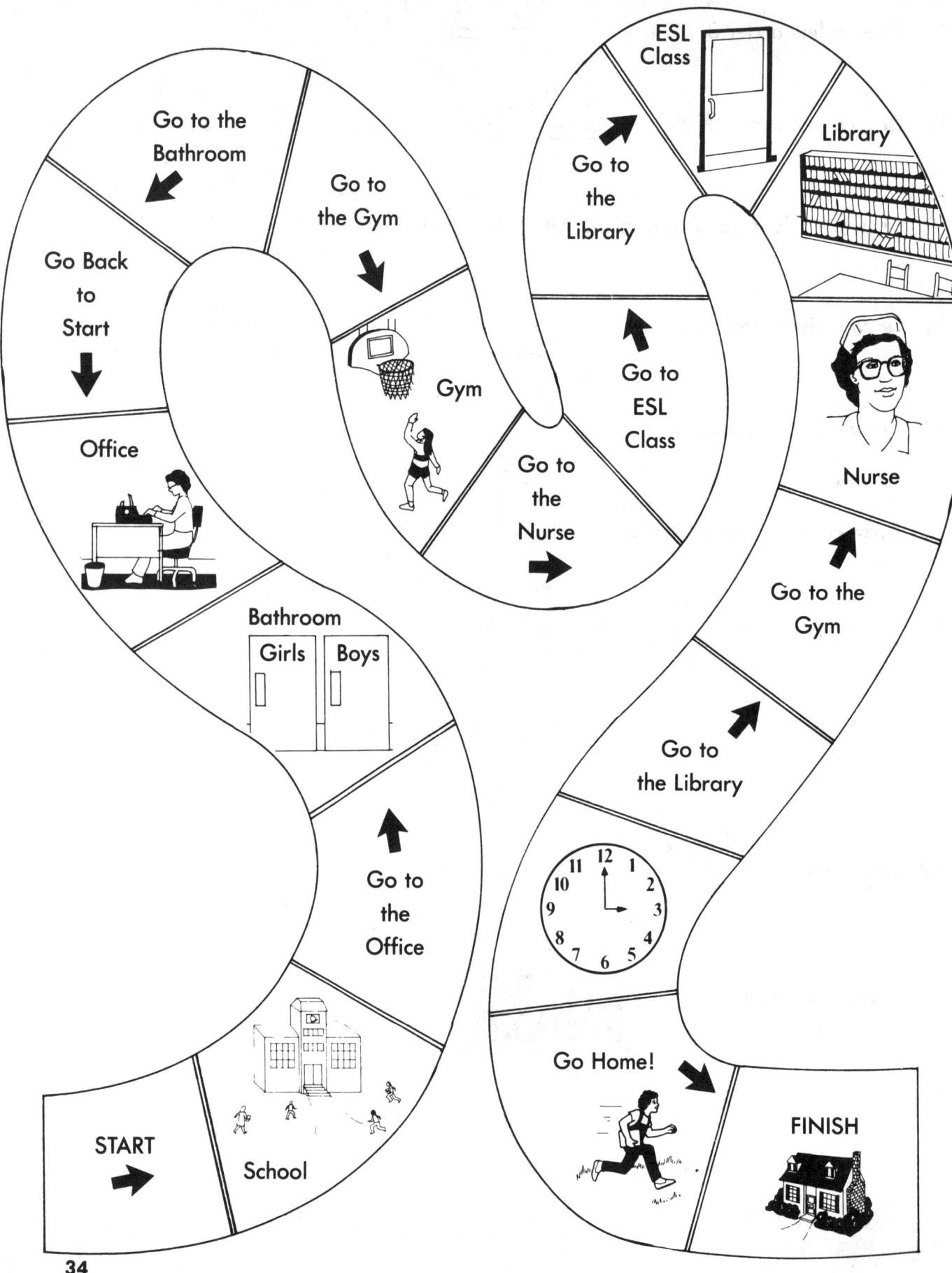

COLORS

COLOR

1. red
2. blue
3. yellow
4. green
5. orange
6. purple
7. black
8. brown
9. white
10. pink

COLOR THE PICTURE

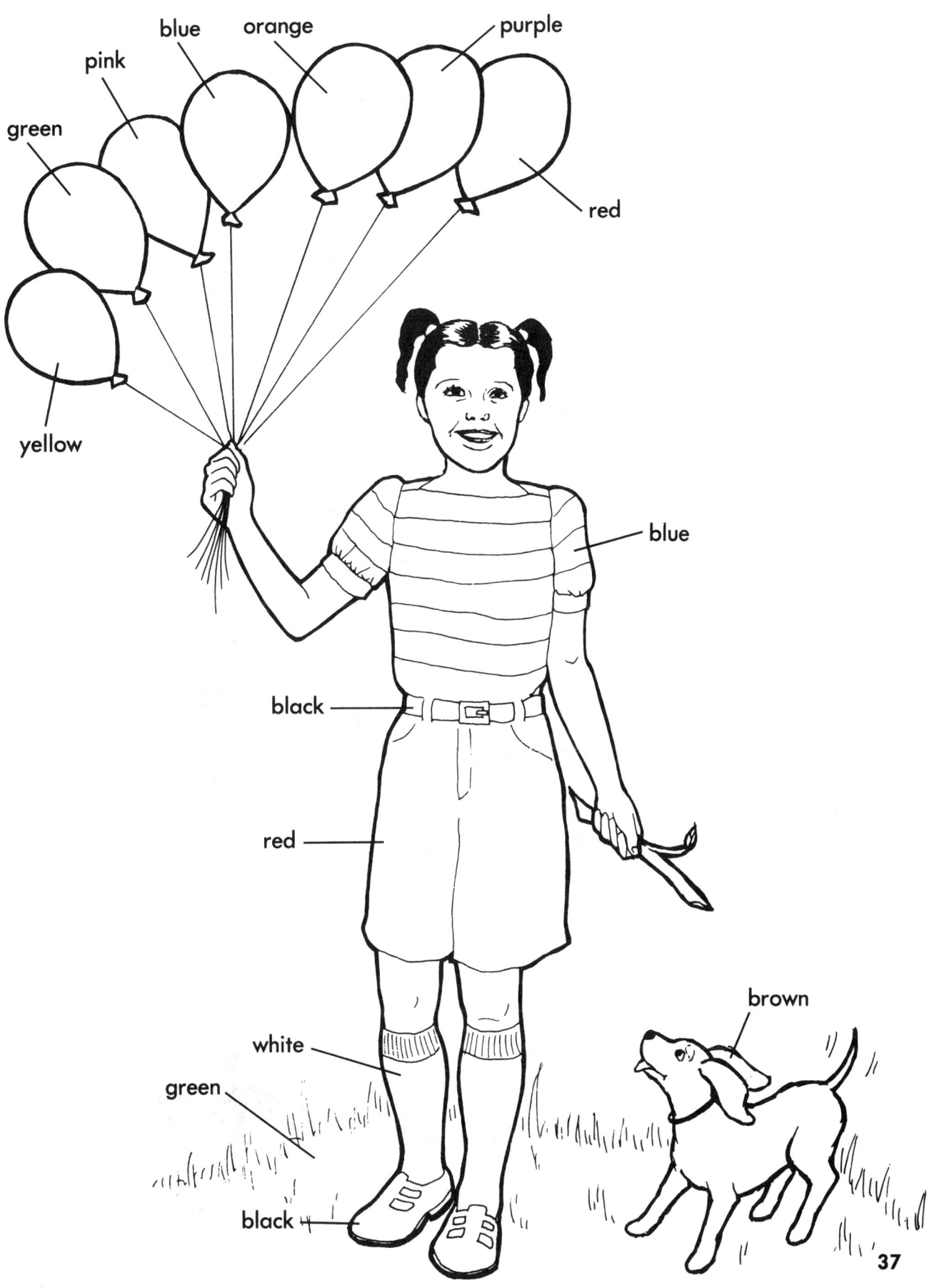

LISTEN

1. Run.

2. Don't run!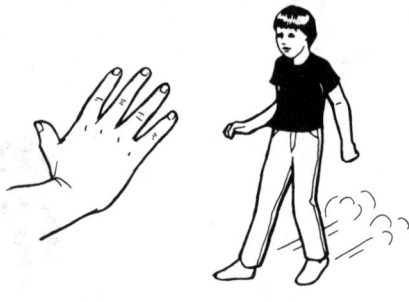

3. Walk.

4. Don't walk.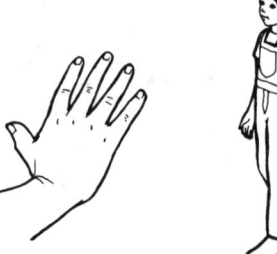

5. Push.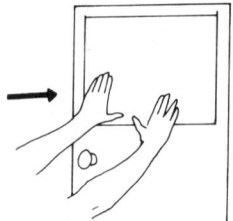

6. Don't push.

7. Hit.

8. Don't hit.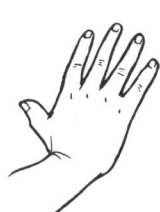

9. Talk.

10. Don't talk.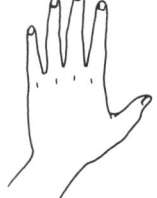

11. Laugh.

12. Don't laugh.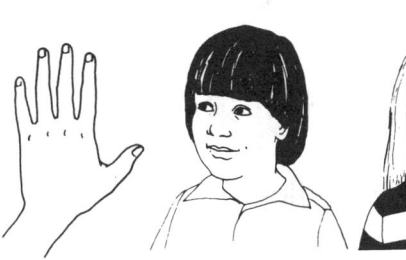

LISTEN AND READ

Draw a circle around the word the teacher says:

1. Hi.   Hello.   So long.   Goodbye.

2. What's your name?

3. My name is Alex.

4. Where are you from?

5. I'm from Japan.

6. This is me.

7. What is it?

8. 5   6   7   8   9

9. 11   12   13   14   15   16

10. Good morning.   Good afternoon.

11. See you tomorrow.

12. Mr.   Miss   Mrs.   Ms.

13. teacher   pen   book   crayon

14. red   yellow   blue   green

15. table   chair   girl   door

16. desk   boy   pencil   flag

THE FACE

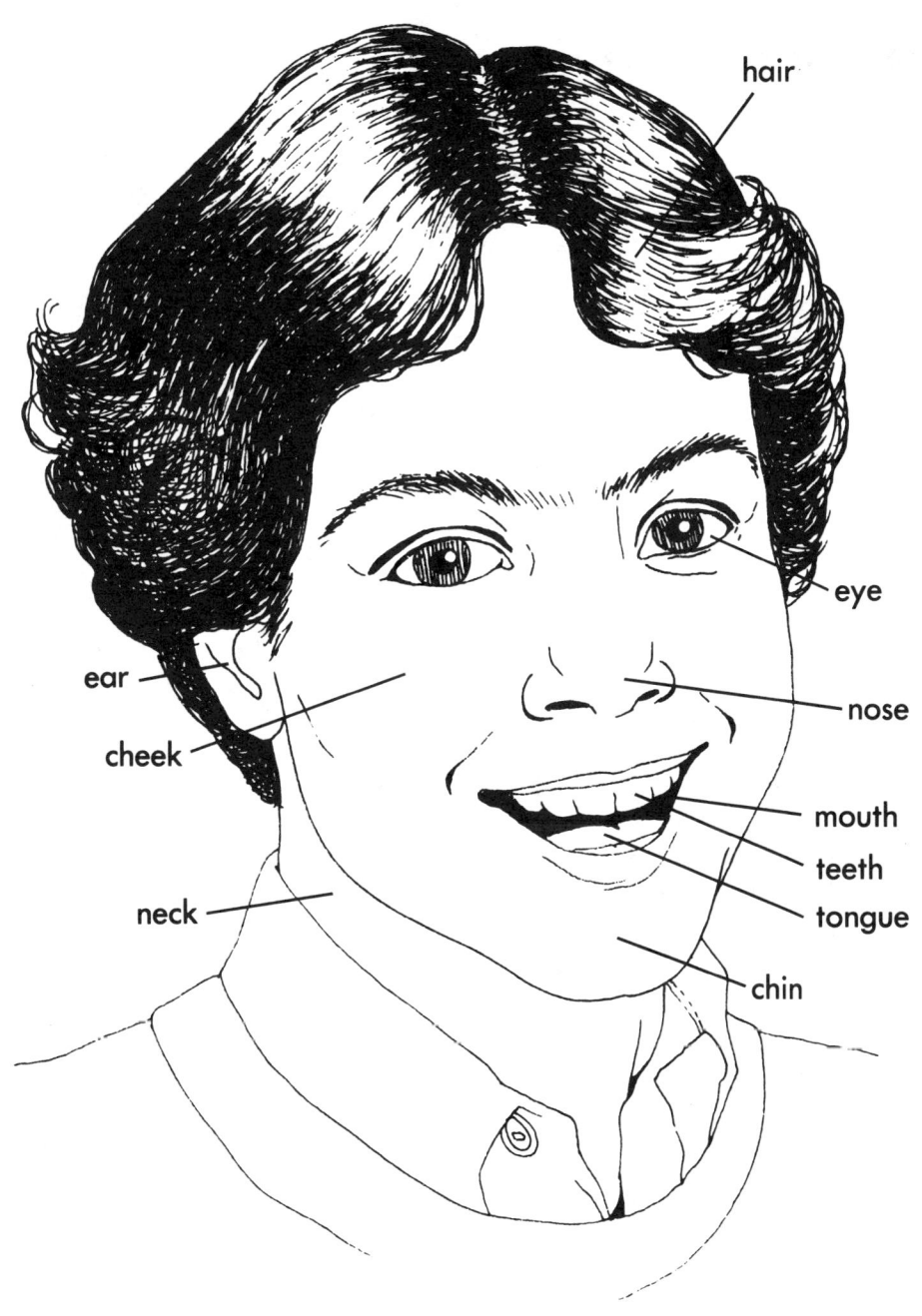

Copy:

hair _____   cheek _____

nose _____   tongue _____

teeth _____   ear _____

neck _____   mouth _____

eye _____   chin _____

DRAW A FACE

Write the names for the parts of the face.

THE BODY

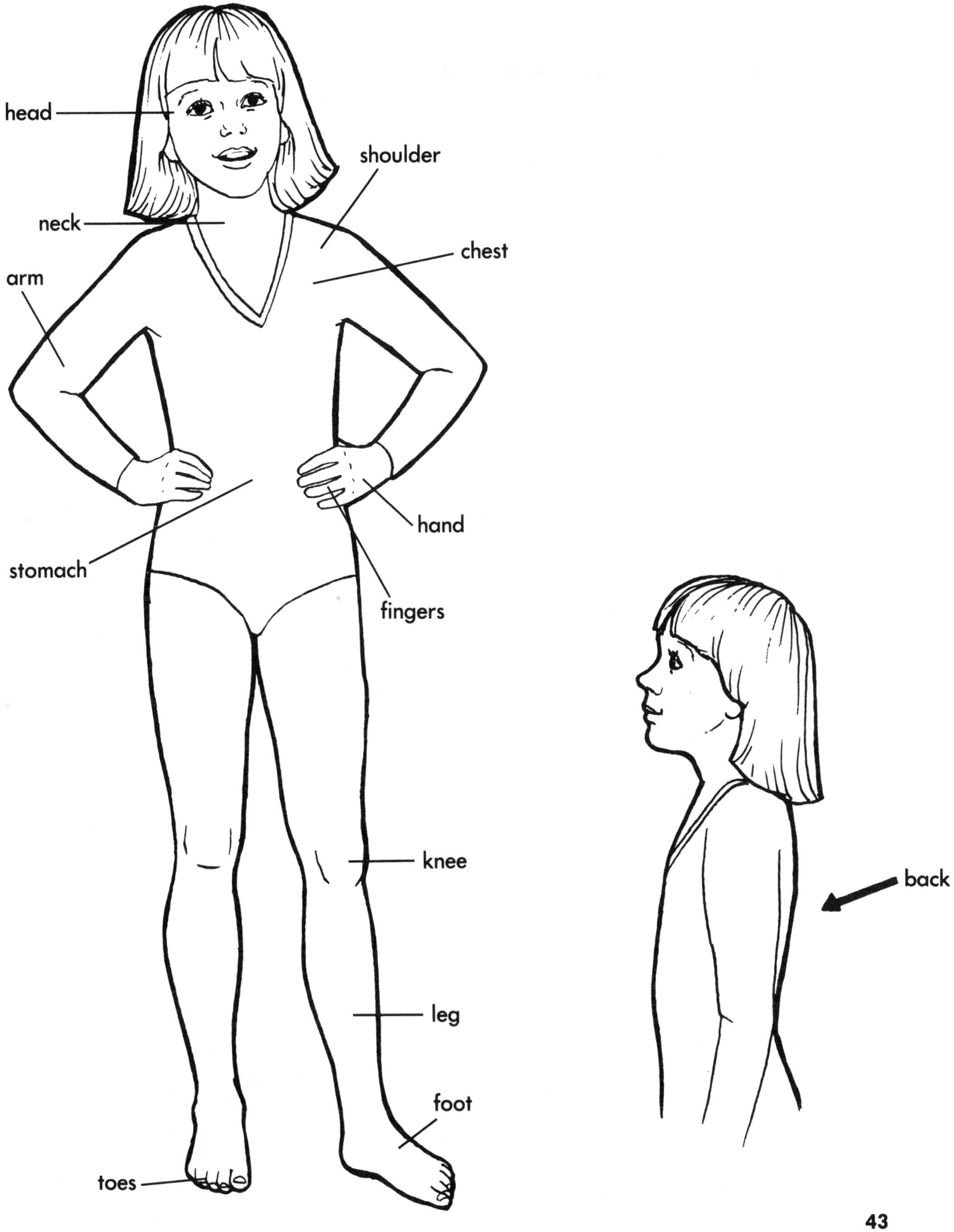

- head
- shoulder
- neck
- chest
- arm
- hand
- stomach
- fingers
- knee
- leg
- foot
- toes
- back

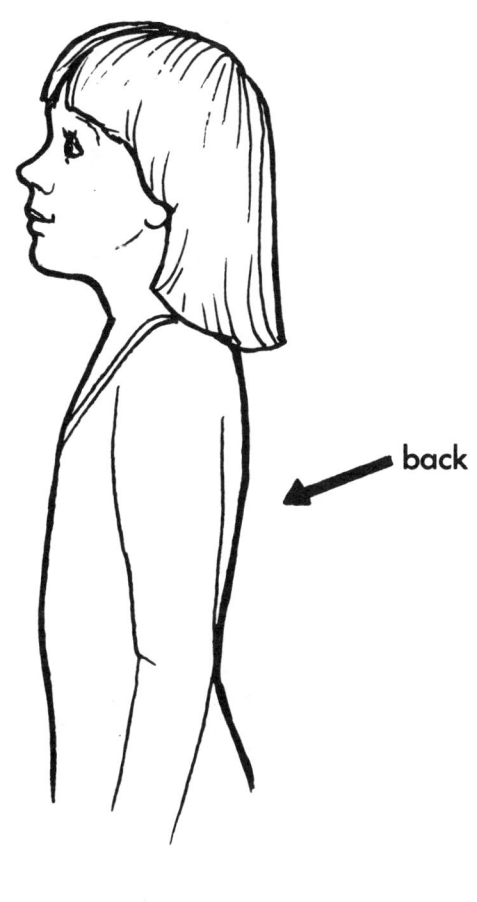

43

DRAW A BOY OR A GIRL

Write the names for the parts of the body.

FIND-A-WORD PUZZLE:
Parts of the Body

Look at the puzzle. Can you find 15 parts of the body? Draw a circle around the words you find. Look ACROSS (⟶) and DOWN (↓).

```
S H O U T O N G U E A S
H K H A N D E T S O H L
O N A M H A C H I N A R
U E N O F R K L E S I N
L E G U E M B A C K R E
D A A T E F I N G E R C
E A R H T O O T H A I T
R I N O S E Y E F O O M
```

1. shoulder
2. ear
3. hand
4. knee
5. back
6. feet
7. tooth
8. eye
9. neck
10. tongue
11. mouth
12. chin
13. nose
14. finger
15. hair

BINGO

		FREE		

Write one word in each square. Mix the order of the words so that everyone's bingo card is different. Cover the words that the teacher says. When you have five words in a row, say "BINGO!"

face	hand	back	tongue
body	finger	eye	mouth
neck	toe	nose	hair
shoulder	foot	chin	head
arm	feet	cheek	knee
leg	chest	ear	stomach

SINGULAR ONE (1)		PLURAL MORE THAN ONE (1+)	
1. man		men	
2. woman		women	
3. child		children	
4. tooth		teeth	
5. foot		feet	
6. eye		eyes	
7. ear		ears	
8. hand		hands	
9. arm		arms	
10. leg		legs	

MATCH

1. ear _____

2. hair _____

3. eyes _____

4. nose _____

5. chin _____

6. tooth _____

7. teeth _____

A.

B.

C.

D.

E.

F.

G.

MATCH

1. back _____

2. shoulder _____

3. hands _____

4. feet _____

5. arm _____

6. finger _____

7. leg _____

8. neck _____

A.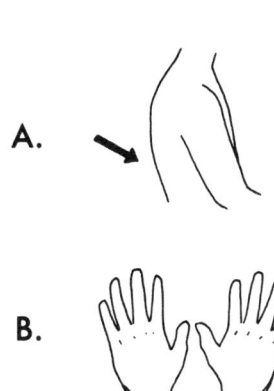

B.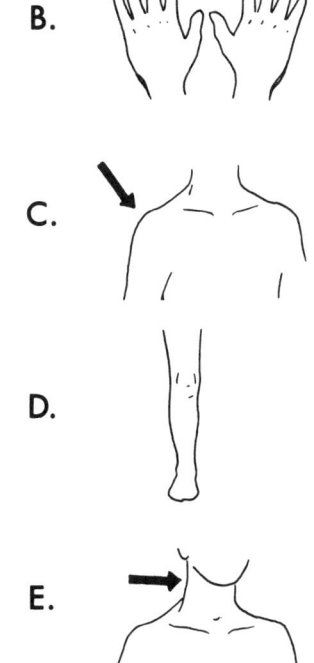

C.

D.

E.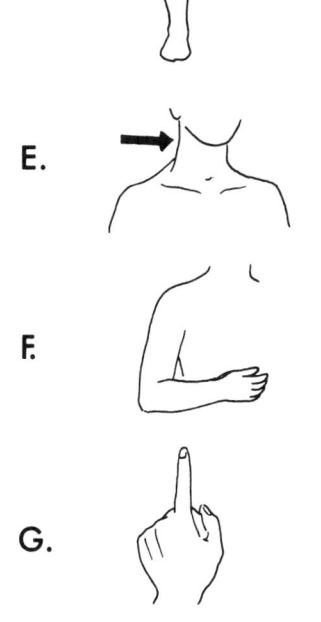

F.

G.

H.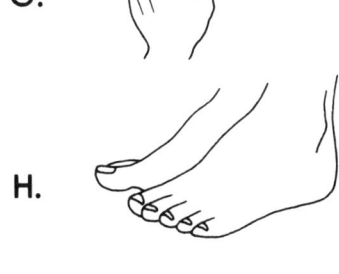

ABC ORDER #1

Write these words in ABC order:

hi	alphabet	copy	English
flag	draw	your	raise
goodbye	is	write	small
knee	language	my	office
pen	name	teacher	United States
book			

a. _____

b. _____

c. _____

d. _____

e. _____

f. _____

g. _____

h. _____

i. _____

j. _____

k. _____

l. _____

m. _____

n. _____

o. _____

p. _____

q. _____

r. _____

s. _____

t. _____

u. _____

v. _____

w. _____

x. _____

y. _____

z. _____

ABC ORDER #2

Write these words in ABC order:

blackboard	door	crayon	yellow
afternoon	morning	notebook	I
eraser	floor	girl	paper
hello	lunch	orange	what
ruler	see	tomorrow	
up			

a. _____

b. _____

c. _____

d. _____

e. _____

f. _____

g. _____

h. _____

i. _____

j. _____

k. _____

l. _____

m. _____

n. _____

o. _____

p. _____

q. _____

r. _____

s. _____

t. _____

u. _____

v. _____

w. _____

x. _____

y. _____

z. _____

ABC ORDER #3

Write these words in ABC order:

nurse	you	under	run
eyes	children	and	dictionary
mouth	hand	foot	laugh
table	window	scissors	

a. _____

b. _____

c. _____

d. _____

e. _____

f. _____

g. _____

h. _____

i. _____

j. _____

k. _____

l. _____

m. _____

n. _____

o. _____

p. _____

q. _____

r. _____

s. _____

t. _____

u. _____

v. _____

w. _____

x. _____

y. _____

z. _____

WRITING NUMBERS

Copy:

0. zero

1. one

2. two

3. three

4. four

5. five

6. six

7. seven

8. eight

9. nine

10. ten

WRITING NUMBERS

Copy:

11. eleven

12. twelve

13. thirteen

14. fourteen

15. fifteen

16. sixteen

17. seventeen

18. eighteen

19. nineteen

20. twenty

21. twenty-one

30. thirty

WRITE THE NUMBER

a. six _6_

c. five _____

e. one _____

g. four _____

i. zero _____

k. twelve _____

m. eleven _____

o. twenty _____

q. sixteen _____

s. eighteen _____

u. nineteen _____

b. eleven _____

d. nine _____

f. three _____

h. eight _____

j. ten _____

l. fifteen _____

n. seventeen _____

p. thirteen _____

r. fourteen _____

t. twenty-two _____

v. thirty _____

WHAT TIME IS IT?

1. What time is it?  It is one o'clock.

2. What time is it?  It's three o'clock.

3. What time is it?  It's six o'clock.

4. What time is it?  It's eight o'clock.

5. What time is it? 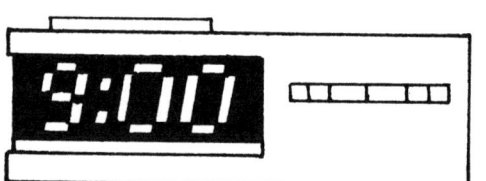 It's nine o'clock.

WHAT TIME IS IT?

There are sixty minutes in one hour.

It's 3:01 (three oh one)   3:05 (three oh five)   3:10 (three ten)   3:15

3:20    3:30    3:35    3:45

3:50    3:55    4 o'clock    4:01

Listen, then draw the hands on the clocks:

THE CALENDAR

OCTOBER

Sunday	Monday	Tuesday	Wednesday	Thursday	Friday	Saturday
		1	2	3	4	5
6	7	8	9	10	11	12
13	14	15	16	17	18	19
20	21	22	23	24	25	26
27	28	29	30	31		

What are the days of the week?

_____

_____

THE DAYS OF THE WEEK

Write the day that is missing:

1. Sunday _____ Tuesday

2. Tuesday _____ Thursday

3. Thursday _____ Saturday

4. Saturday _____ Monday

5. Monday _____ Wednesday

6. Wednesday _____ Friday

7. Friday _____ Sunday

Write the missing letter:

8. S__nday

9. Mo__day

10. Tu__sday

11. We__nesday

12. Thu__sday

13. Fr__day

14. Sa__urday

Make a calendar for this month.

1. What is the month? _____

2. What is the year? _____

3. What day of the week is today? _____

4. What day is tomorrow? _____

5. What day was yesterday? _____

6. What is the date? _____

REVIEW

QUESTIONS

1. What's your name? _____
2. What's your last name? _____
3. How are you? _____
4. What day is today? _____
5. Where are you from? _____
6. What are the days of the week? _____
7. May I go to the bathroom please? _____

ANSWERS

A. I'm fine, thank you.

B. Yes, you may.

C. My name is Jack.

D. Sunday, Monday, Tuesday, Wednesday, Thursday, Friday, Saturday.

E. I'm from Japan.

F. Today is Friday, October 10.

G. My last name is Lee.

QUESTIONS AND ANSWERS

What's your telephone number?

Where do you live?

What's your address?

My telephone number is 123-4567.

I live at 1025 Center Street.

1025 Center Street, Apartment 3-B
Nicetown, New Jersey
07662

Answer:

1. What's your telephone number?

My telephone number is _____.

2. Where do you live?

I live at _____

_____

Draw a picture of your house:
This is my house.

ADDRESS A LETTER

1. To your teacher:

   Name _____
   Number and Street _____
   Town, State _____
   Zip Code _____

2. To your mother and father at home:

MATCH

1. drawer _____
2. bookcase _____
3. box _____
4. dictionary _____
5. pencil sharpener _____
6. tape recorder _____
7. headphones _____
8. paste _____
9. ruler _____
10. picture _____

A.
B.
C.
D.
E.
F.
G.
H.
I.
J.

LISTEN

1. Look!

2. Look at the blackboard.

3. Look at the picture.

4. Look at the alphabet.  a b c d e f g h i j k l m
   n o p q r s t u v w x y z

5. Look up.

6. Look down.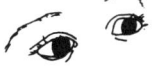

7. Look at me.

8. Point to the blackboard.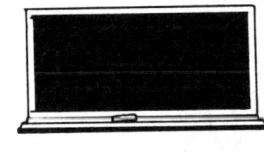

9. Point to the picture.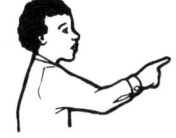

10. Point to the door.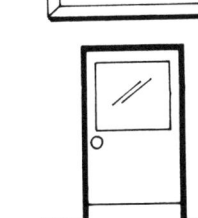

11. Point to the bookcase

12. Point to the wastebasket.

WHAT DO YOU SEE?

Look at the picture. Write yes or no:

1. Do you see a teacher? _____

2. Do you see children? _____

3. Do you see a dog? _____

4. Do you see a calendar? _____

5. Do you see a nurse? _____

6. What else do you see?

1. _____
2. _____
3. _____
4. _____
5. _____
6. _____
7. _____
8. _____
9. _____
10. _____
11. _____
12. _____
13. _____
14. _____
15. _____
16. _____
17. _____
18. _____
19. _____
20. _____
21. _____
22. _____

LISTEN

1. Look in the box.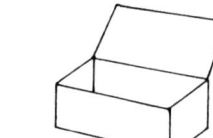

2. Give me the ruler, please.

3. Give me the scissors, please.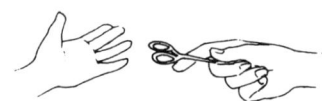

4. Give me the dictionary, please.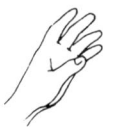

5. Give me the paste, please.

6. Give me the chalk, please.

7. Give me three pencils, please.

8. Give me two erasers, please.

9. Give me the blue crayon, please.

10. Give me the brown crayon and the yellow crayon, please.

11. Give me the red crayon, the yellow crayon and the black crayon, please.

MORE QUESTIONS AND ANSWERS

1. How old are you? — I'm nine years old.

2. How old are you? — I'm ten years old.

3. How old are you? — I'm eleven years old.

4. How old are you? — I'm _____ years old.

first   second   third   fourth   fifth   sixth

5. What grade are you in? — I'm in the fourth grade.

6. What grade are you in? — I'm in the fifth grade.

7. What grade are you in? — I'm in the sixth grade.

8. What grade are you in? — I'm in the _____ grade.

71

1. Who is your teacher? My teacher is Miss Day.

Miss Day

2. Who is your teacher? My teacher is Mrs. Land.

Mrs. Land

3. Who is your teacher? My teacher is Mr. Hill.

Mr. Hill

4. Who is your teacher? My teacher is _____.

5. Who is your friend? My friend is Tom.

Tom

6. Who is your friend? My friend is Milly.

Milly

7. Who is your friend? My friend is Jack.

Jack

8. Who is your friend? My friend is _____.

COPY

1. How old are you?

   _____

2. I'm _____ years old.

   _____

3. What grade are you in?

   _____

4. I am in the _____ grade.

   _____

5. Who is your teacher?

   _____

6. My teacher is _____.

   _____

WRITE ABOUT YOURSELF

My name is _____. I am from

_____. I am _____ years old. I am in the

_____ grade. My teacher is _____.

I live at _____.

My telephone number is _____.

Copy the story:

_____

_____

_____

_____

_____

_____

HOW ARE YOU?

Look at the pictures. Write the answers.

1. Who is sad? _Tom is sad._
2. Who is sick? _____
3. Who is tired? _____
4. Who is happy? _____
5. Who is angry? _____
6. Who is absent? _____

Fill in the blanks:

1. Who is thirsty? _____ and _____ are thirsty.
2. Who is hot? _____ and _____ are hot.
3. Who is cold? _____, _____, and _____ are cold.
4. Who is hungry? _____ and _____ are hungry.

PRONOUNS

(person)	I	We	(two people)
	You		
(man)	He	They	(two men)
(woman)	She	They	(two women)
(chair)	It	They	(three chairs)

Write the correct pronoun:

1. My name is Tom. _____ am from Japan.
2. Milly is cold. _____ is hungry too.
3. _____ are from the U.S.A. _____ are American.
4. Jack is sad. _____ is sick.
5. How are _____? _____ 'm fine, thank you.
6. This is a book. _____ is my book.
7. Look at the dogs. _____ are hungry.
8. Are you in the fourth grade? No, _____ are in the fifth grade.
9. Miss Day and Mrs. Land are teachers. _____ are American.

AM, IS, ARE

I am late.		We are late.
		You are late.
He is late.		They are late.
She is late.		
It is late.		
One person is late.		Many people are late.

How many sentences can you make?

I	am	late.
He She Linda The dog	is	early. hungry. thirsty. from Japan.
We You The boys Jack and Jimmy	are	cold. hot. nine years old. from the U.S.A.

YES, I AM. OR NO, I'M NOT.

1. Are you from Japan?
   _____

2. Are you sick today?
   _____

3. Are you absent today?
   _____

4. Are you hungry?
   _____

5. Are you thirsty?
   _____

6. Are you hot?
   _____

7. Are you cold?
   _____

8. Are you happy?
   _____

TOYS

1. car

2. ball

3. doll

4. balloon

5. train

6. dog

7. cat

8. puppet

9. bicycle

SINGULAR OR PLURAL
(ONE) OR (MORE THAN ONE)

Listen to the teacher. Draw a circle around the correct picture.

Now, draw a circle around the correct word.

9. dog   dogs
10. picture   pictures
11. bicycle   bicycles
12. desk   desks

13. car   cars
14. ball   balls
15. ruler   rulers
16. class   classes

WHAT DO YOU HAVE?

1. What do you have?　　　　　　　　　　I have a car.

2. What do you have?　　　　　　　　　　I have two cars.

3. What do you have?　　　　　　　　　　I have a balloon.

4. What do you have?　　　　　　　　　　I have three balloons.

5. I have a doll.　　　　　　　　　　　　I have two dolls.

6. I have a puppet.　　　　　　　　　　　I have two puppets.

7. I have a dog.　　　　　　　　　　　　I have two dogs.

8. I have a cat.　　　　　　　　　　　　I have many cats.

HOW MANY?

Write the answers in complete sentences.

1. How many pencils do you have?

   _____

2. How many pens do you have?

   _____

3. How many books do you have?

   _____

4. How many eyes do you have?

   _____

5. How many fingers do you have?

   _____

6. How many teeth do you have?

   _____

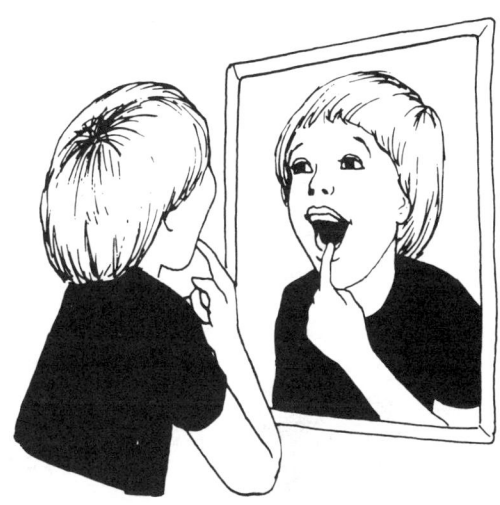

DO YOU HAVE _____?

1. Do you have a ruler?  Yes, I have a ruler.

2. Do you have a dictionary?  No, I don't have a dictionary.

3. Do you have a balloon?  No, I don't have a balloon.

4. Do you have a dog?  No, I don't have a dog.

5. Do you have a cat?  Yes, I have a cat.

6. Do you have a notebook? 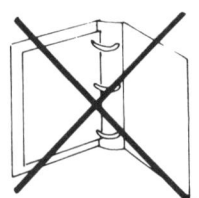 No, I don't have a notebook.

7. Do you have a tape recorder? 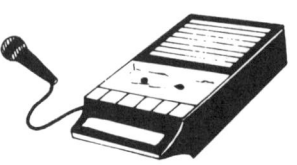 Yes, I have a tape recorder.

8. Do you have a telephone?  No, I don't have a telephone.

1. Do you have a dog?

2. Do you have a cat?

3. Do you have a dictionary?

4. Do you have a bicycle?

5. Do you have a doll?

6. Do you have black hair?

7. Do you have blue eyes?

8. Do you have green fingers?

MILLY'S FAMILY

1. This is my mother.
   Her name is Maria.

2. This is my father.
   His name is John.

3. This is my sister.
   Her name is Linda.

4. This is my brother.
   His name is Jimmy.

5. This is my grandmother.
   Her name is Nan.

6. This is my grandfather.
   His name is Bob.

THIS IS MY FAMILY

Draw your family:

1. This is me. My name is _____

2. This is my _____

3. _____

4. _____

5. _____

6. _____

ASK QUESTIONS

Talk to a boy. Ask these questions. Write the answers.

1. What is your last name? _____

2. Where are you from? _____

3. How old are you? _____

4. What grade are you in? _____

5. Who is your teacher? _____

6. Do you have any brothers? _____ How many? _____

7. Do you have any sisters? _____ How many? _____

Talk to a girl. Ask these questions:

1. What is your last name? _____

2. Where are you from? _____

3. How old are you? _____

4. What grade are you in? _____

5. Who is your teacher? _____

6. Do you have any brothers? _____ How many? _____

7. Do you have any sisters? _____ How many? _____

Write about a boy:

This is my friend _____.
His last name is _____.
He is from _____. He is
_____ years old. He is in the _____ grade.
He has _____ brother__ and _____ sister__.

Copy the story:

_____

_____

_____

_____

_____

_____

_____

_____

Read the story to the class.

Write about a girl:

This is my friend _____.
Her last name is _____.
She is from _____. She is
_____ years old. She is in the _____ grade.
She has _____ brother __ and _____ sister __.

Copy the story:

_____

_____

_____

_____

_____

_____

Read the story to the class.

LISTEN

1. Go to the blackboard.   Bring me a ruler.

2. Go to the blackboard.   Bring me an eraser.

3. Go to the blackboard.   Bring me some chalk.

4. Go to the teacher's desk.   Bring me two pencils and an eraser.

5. Go to the teacher's desk.   Bring me a pair of scissors.

6. Go to the teacher's desk.   Bring me some paper.

7. Go to the bookcase.   Bring me a dictionary and four books.

8. Go to the bookcase.   Bring me some paste and a box of crayons.

9. Go to the bookcase.   Bring me a tape recorder and some headphones.

MORE NUMBERS

10 ten _____ 60 sixty _____
20 twenty _____ 70 seventy _____
30 thirty _____ 80 eighty _____
40 forty _____ 90 ninety _____
50 fifty _____ 100 one hundred _____

1. Count by two's to thirty.
2. Count by three's to thirty.
3. Count by ten's to one hundred.
4. Count by five's to one hundred.
5. Read these numbers:

   a. 47   52   35   61   78   97   54   23
   b. 23   54   67   89   12   39   40   11
   c. 51   60   39   68   27   15   26   53
   d. 123   135   156   267   289   207
   e. 342   378   498   470   506   699
   f. 177   888   654   321   670   201

6. Write these numbers:

   a. fifty-one _____   f. two hundred _____
   b. seventy-three _____   g. three hundred two _____
   c. forty-nine _____   h. six hundred nineteen _____
   d. thirty-seven _____   i. eight hundred thirty-one _____
   e. eighty-two _____   j. nine hundred fifteen _____

MONEY

   one dollar $1.00

   half dollar   (fifty cents)   50 ¢ $.50

   quarter   (twenty-five cents)   25 ¢ $.25

   dime   (ten cents)   10 ¢ $.10

   nickel   (five cents)   5 ¢ $.05

   penny   (one cent)   1 ¢ $.01

MONEY: MATCH

1. quarter   (dime image)   10¢

2. dime   (half dollar image)   1¢

3. nickel   (nickel image)   5¢

4. penny   (penny image)   50¢

5. half dollar   (quarter image)   25¢

How much is it?

_____

_____

_____

HOW MUCH IS IT?
(COIN EXERCISES)

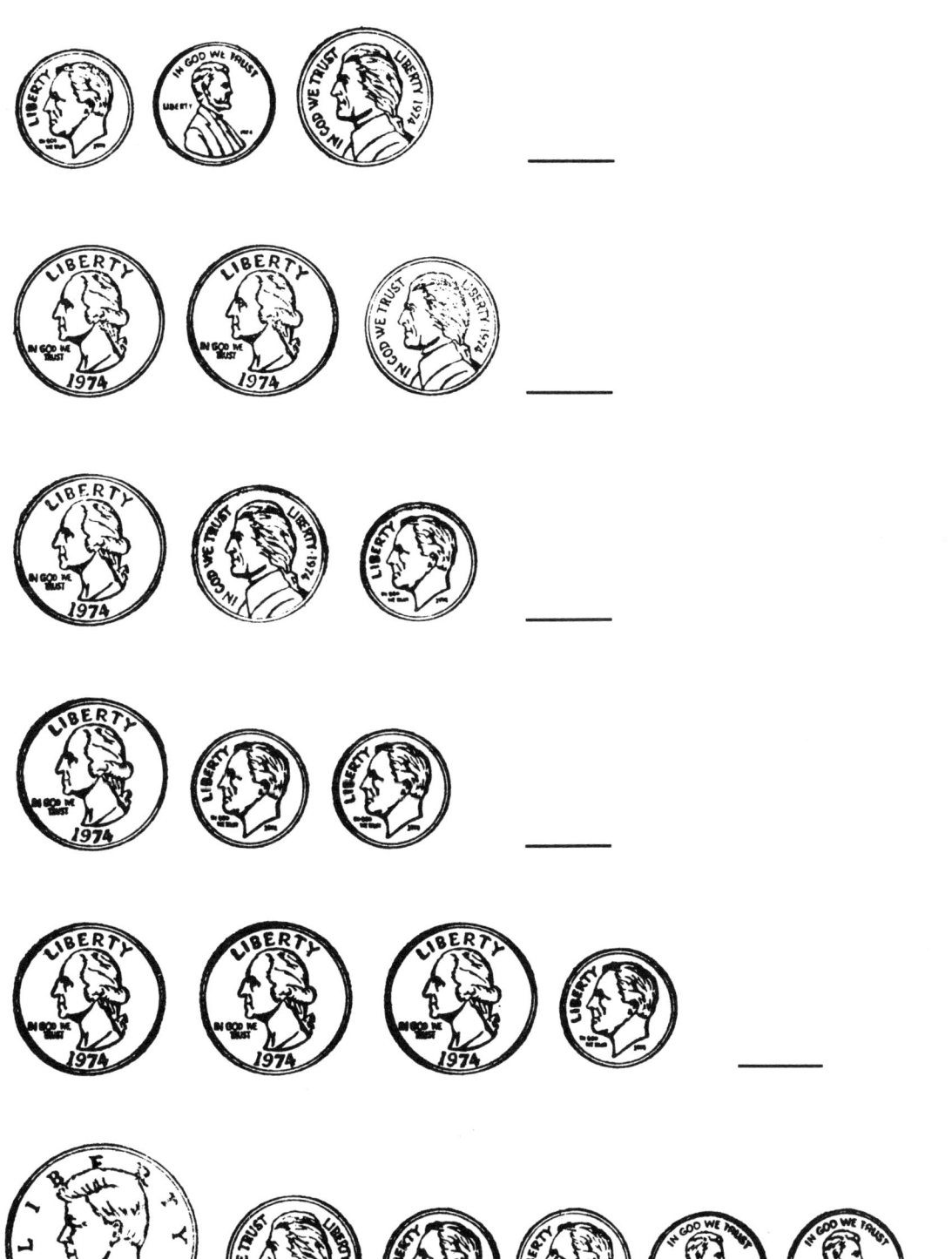

CONVERSATION REVIEW

Answer these questions in complete sentences:

1. What's your name? _____

2. What's your last name? _____

3. How are you? _____

4. Where are you from? _____

5. Where do you live? _____

   _____

6. Who is your teacher? _____

7. What grade are you in? _____

8. How old are you? _____

9. What day is today? _____

10. Are you thirsty? _____

REVIEW

1. Write the days of the week:

   _____   _____

   _____   _____

   _____   _____

   _____

2. Write the names of people in your class:

   _____   _____

   _____   _____

   _____   _____

   _____   _____

   _____   _____

3. Write these numbers:

   6 _____   14 _____

   3 _____   20 _____

   8 _____   45 _____

   12 _____   31 _____

   11 _____   59 _____

4. Write ten colors:

_____   _____

_____   _____

_____   _____

_____   _____

_____   _____

5. Write fifteen parts of the body:

_____   _____

_____   _____

_____   _____

_____   _____

_____   _____

_____   _____

_____   _____

_____

6. Write six places in the school:

_____   _____

_____   _____

_____   _____

7. Write twelve things you can find in a classroom:

_____ _____

_____ _____

_____ _____

_____ _____

_____ _____

_____ _____

8. Write ten toys:

_____ _____

_____ _____

_____ _____

_____ _____

_____ _____

9. Write the names of six people in a family:

_____ _____

_____ _____

_____ _____

10. What coins are these?

five cents _____   ten cents _____

one cent _____   fifty cents _____

twenty-five cents _____

REVIEW: SENTENCE STRUCTURE

Choose the correct word:

1. I _____ from China. (am, is, are)

2. My sister _____ hungry. (am, is, are)

3. My father and mother _____ happy. (am, is, are)

4. How old _____ you? (am, is, are)

5. _____ your friends sad today? (am, is, are)

6. _____ color is chalk? (What, Where, How)

7. Where are the rulers? _____ are in the desk. (They, It, It's)

8. Where _____ you live? (is, are, do)

9. _____ you have a sister? (Are, Do, Does)

10. Yes, I _____ a sister. (have, has, am)

REVIEW: VOCABULARY

Read the four words in each row. Three words go together. One word is different. Draw a circle around the word that does not belong with the other words.

1. seven — twelve — yellow — thirteen
2. red — orange — blue — chin
3. foot — ear — nose — mouth
4. Sunday — January — Tuesday — Thursday
5. table — pen — crayon — pencil
6. mother — sister — father — teacher
7. run — walk — don't — go
8. notebook — write — listen — read
9. library — lunch — office — classroom
10. Mr. — Miss — Mrs. — my
11. they — am — she — it
12. what — white — who — where
13. hand — finger — arm — dictionary
14. dog — boy — girl — woman
15. please — thank you — you're welcome — goodbye
16. boy — bicycle — ball — balloon
17. his — her — I — your
18. dollar — nickel — penny — doll
19. nurse — principal — child — teacher
20. hungry — cat — thirsty — tired

WRITE A STORY

Write about: You, your class, or your family and friends.

BE POLITE

THE FLAG SALUTE

I pledge allegiance
to the Flag
of the United States of America
and to the Republic
for which it stands;
one nation, under God
indivisible,
with liberty and justice for all.

AMERICA

My country 'tis of thee
Sweet land of liberty
Of thee I sing
Land where my fathers died
Land of the Pilgrim's pride
From every mountainside
Let freedom ring.